Preface:

One of the main reasons I took on the challenge of writing this book is that I am concerned about the lack of leadership I have observed in the last 10 years. In general terms, it seems that leaders today are more concerned about bettering themselves as opposed to bettering their organizations. From the 2008 financial crisis to the 2013 government shutdown, which is on day 13 as I write this paragraph, too many bad situations take place because of personal greed and ego.

I graduated from the United States Military Academy in 1997. As of this writing, my classmates who remained in the Army are pinning on Lieutenant Colonel, a significant milestone for officers, and those who got out are serving in other government agencies or serving in the business community. No matter which path they chose, all are still committed to serving others. I have had the tremendous experience of working with great selfless leaders who put themselves last and truly worked for the greater good. I know there are more out there who share these values. I recently had the pleasure of meeting Seth Goldman, Tea EO of Honest Tea, who spoke about the importance of being a values based organization, promoting fair wages for the undeveloped world while marketing a healthy product. There are also countless selfless soldiers and civilians, many of whom I have met and worked with first hand, who work tirelessly around the world to keep our nation safe. These people I mentioned above all share a common ethos. I try to capture the essence of that ethos in my book while also sharing some valuable lessons you can apply to better your organization and yourself starting today.

As you read through these lessons, keep in mind that there is so much we can learn from history. Sometimes we are too quick to dismiss something historical because it does not relate to our modern age given the advances in technology. Leading, however, has always been about people. The methods we use to communicate may change, but the fundamentals do not. For instance, the Civil War was the first war that incorporated the telegraph, which allowed commanders the ability to communicate at greater distances than previously possible. However, even technology cannot replace human interaction. We are social creatures and that will never change.

Regarding the situations and dynamics that took place during the Battle of Gettysburg, I relied on "Gettysburg a Day by Day Account of the Greatest Battle of the Civil War," edited by Kelly Knauer and published by Time Warner Entertainment, 2013. It is a great summary of the key points in this battle. The book cover is sourced to the Library of Congress and also appeared in the Bangor Daily News. The leadership lessons I extract from these battlefield accounts are lessons I obtained from my classes at West Point and battlefield tours I took as an Army Officer. I have also taken lessons from my own personal experiences and added those for the reader.

I want to dedicate this book to selfless leaders and individuals everywhere, particularly Mark Mensack, my longtime mentor and friend. Mark was a former Army Officer, West Point professor, and has been a financial advisor for the last 17 years. He was a whistle blower against Morgan Stanley's unethical sales practices and has been vindicated by an investigation which has almost neared conclusion. He went through tremendous financial and personal turmoil during this ordeal; despite all this, he maintained a positive outlook and never gave up. He is one of the best modern examples of a leader who is willing to do the right thing regardless of the personal consequences. I also dedicate this book to you, the reader. My hope is that you are inspired by these examples and that you strive to be a servant leader. Finally, I want to thank my wife, Isabel, for all the hard work and dedication she demonstrates daily. She also spent countless hours editing this book and without her love and support, I could not have finished this book.

Thanks for buying this book and good luck on your successes.

Introduction:

The battle of Gettysburg is considered to be the greatest battle of the American Civil War and it was the costliest battle in terms of casualties in North America. With the 150th anniversary of Gettysburg, tourists will flock to this National Park to understand the battle and the significance it had on the fate of our country. However, understanding Gettysburg is more than just understanding military history, weapons, and tactics. It is about people. People on both sides who fought for a cause they believed in and were willing to die for. When it comes to people, the most important aspects of interacting with people are leadership, teamwork, trust, and most importantly, communication. Without proper communication, you cannot lead or build your team, lay a foundation of trust, or complete your task. As I will demonstrate in this book, poor communication is one of the primary reasons Confederate General Robert E. Lee lost at Gettysburg. This book will give you lessons on the importance of effective communication; lessons you can use to make you more effective in leading your team. If you are not a historian, do not worry, you do not have to be an expert on the battle. The pertinent points of the battle are mentioned to serve as a backdrop for the lessons. So now let's journey back to those three bloody days from July 1 to 3, 1863, and learn the art of communication and leadership.

Chapter 1: The Importance of knowing your Communication Style (First, know thyself)

Many people have never heard of General George Gordon Meade, the victorious general at the Battle of Gettysburg. Among Union Army generals, he is overshadowed by well known victorious generals Ulysses S. Grant and General William T. Sherman. Even failed Union generals have more fame than he. Meade's opponent, Robert E. Lee, was without a doubt one of the most famous generals in history. President Abraham Lincoln had originally asked Lee to take command of the Union Army, but Lee refused on the basis that he could not fight against his home state of Virginia. Meade, on the other hand, received the job only because Lincoln lost confidence in previous generals he appointed and more senior generals that were eligible turned the job down. Yet it was Meade who would hand Lee his first defeat at Union hands.

President Abraham Lincoln appointed General George Gordon Meade to command the Army of the Potomac just three days before the Battle of Gettysburg. President Abraham Lincoln selected Meade over other more senior ranking generals after General John F. Reynolds turned down President Lincoln's suggestion he take command. Meade, who was surprised by the appointment and had not actively sought the position, was left to organize his forces relatively quickly. His challenges included lack of expertise, the presence of more senior generals under his command, and the lack of time before he had to confront the Army of Northern Virginia. Meade also was about to lead his first battle as commander of the Army of the Potomac; a team who had constantly lost to the Army of Northern Virginia.

Before he could even start planning his mission to defeat Robert E. Lee and the Army of Northern Virginia, a task no commander had been able to do, General Meade had to assert himself as the commander and ensure his subordinate generals understood his goals and objectives. He accomplished this by consulting with his war council before making decisions. Meade also however made it very clear that ultimately any decision was his and once made, he expected his generals to follow his guidance. Because he was new to his position, Meade provided very clear orders and routinely sent staff officers to make sure units were following his orders.

Confederate general Robert E. Lee, Commander of the Army of Northern Virginia, on the other hand, was arguably the most highly regarded general during the war. Some historians suggest Lee was the best general the United States ever produced. Before the war began, Lincoln offered Lee command of the Union Army; however, Lee would not bring himself to fight against the Commonwealth of Virginia, his birthplace with strong family ties. Leading up to the battle of Gettysburg, Lee pulled off stunning victories against the Army of the Potomac and was therefore, very confident. Lee made all decisions himself and rarely sought the advice of others. Subordinate generals knew to not even offer him advise. However, he also relied on the judgment of his subordinate commanders, particularly General Thomas "Stonewall" Jackson, who understood how Lee thought, and demonstrated superb battlefield skills, thus allowing Lee to provide general guidance, relying then on Jackson to make a decision based on the tactical situation on the ground. This style of leadership is well suited for an organization in which key leaders and team members have worked together for a while and understand how each other thinks and works things out. Although Lee would give Jackson some guidance as opposed to clear cut tasks, Jackson would issue very specific orders to his subordinate commanders.

By the time the attacks at Gettysburg began though, Lee had lost his right hand man, "Stonewall" Jackson. Jackson had not only been Lee's most trusted commander, he was one of the few subordinate commanders to really understand Lee's unstated guidance and intentions. Their relationship was very strong due to the mutual trust developed through their service together. Jackson understood Lee's methodology and the more gentile way of speaking that Lee was known for. Upon observing Jackson's success, Lee relied heavily on Jackson and rarely followed up on his instructions, and instead would await for Jackson to update him. Unfortunately, Jackson was killed by his own troops during the Battle of Chancellorsville. What makes the death even more unfortunate is that it was a result of poor communication. During the night of May 2, 1863, which followed a very successful Confederate battlefield victory, Jackson rode forward with some of his officers to reconnoiter the battlefield. However, he failed to inform the soldiers who secured the perimeter that they were leaving. Upon returning to Confederate lines, nervous Confederate soldiers mistook the group for a Union cavalry patrol and opened fire. Jackson was hit three times and died of his wounds on May 10, 1863. As a result of Jackson's death, Lee not only lost his most reliable commander but faced the challenge of leading with a new, untested team member in a key position.

Lieutenant General Richard S. Ewell replaced Stonewall Jackson as Lee's right-hand and executer of his instructions. Ewell, who had served under Jackson, had less experience than Jackson and was not accustomed to Lee's less direct style of communication. Jackson had been very forceful and direct when issuing orders, leaving nothing to chance. When Ewell took Jackson's place as corps commander, Ewell found himself in the unfamiliar territory of dealing with a senior officer (Lee) who was very gentile and not always direct with his communication style. From the onset of the battle, Lee thus faced the challenge of adapting to a new key team member while leading forces in a hostile and time-sensitive environment.

Lee made the mistake of assuming he could manage Ewell the same way he managed Jackson and achieve the same results. Lee had never worked with Ewell as a corps commander. Even as the battle developed and it became clear that Ewell was incapable of dealing with Lee's ambiguity, Lee never adjusted his communication style to be more direct. As a subordinate, Ewell could also have tried to adapt to Lee's management style by asking more questions to seek clarifications from his supervisor.

As I will outline in more detail later on, this gap in communication, and the unintentional consequences that followed, demonstrate the importance of communication and asking questions. General Lee had the time to sit down with Ewell and learn about him and what made him tick. Lee could also have explained his command philosophy which would have been a help to both Ewell and Lee. However, when he did not, Ewell had the choice of asking more questions from his supervisor; he had the option to manage up.

Neither communication style as applied by Meade and Lee is right or wrong. What is critical in a business setting, and personal setting as well, is that a leader understand the strengths and weaknesses of his or her communication style and engage with his or her staff accordingly. As a subordinate, you can maximize your performance by asking questions from your supervisors, especially if clear information is not forthcoming. In your career, you will find yourself in a position where you may be asked to lead like Meade in an area where you have very little expertise in or you may have to lead, like Lee, with a new team. Meade sought advice from more senior and experienced officers while asserting himself as a competent leader. He also followed up with subordinates to make sure they were understanding his instructions and executing them accordingly. Lee assumed Ewell would adapt to his communication style. Successful leaders come in all shapes and sizes and the key to their success is knowing themselves and being able to adapt to a new working environment. Successful leaders can take on different forms.

Chapter 2: Understanding the picture: the need to train and empower subordinates

Empowering subordinates is very important for the simple fact that leaders cannot be effective if they have to be spend time figuring out every minor detail of a project. Leaders need to shape the outcome with clear guidance; however, they also need to empower subordinates to demonstrate trust, and thus increase initiative and creativity. Ultimately the best managers are able to tap the potential of every employee. Another important point is that your most junior team members are usually closer to the action, and thus in a better position to make more educated and faster decisions than most managers, thus saving time. If junior members constantly have to seek guidance, the decision making process slows down rapidly. As speaker and New York best-selling author Tim Ferris, says in his book The Four Hour Work Week, "It is amazing how much a person's IQ improves when you give them responsibility." The most important guidance you should issue as a leader is "Commander's Intent" or the desired outcome of the planned action. By stating a clear intent, those below you are able to adjust their courses of action when the unexpected happens and still obtain the stated goal. This is exactly what happened to Union General John Buford during the first day of fighting at Gettysburg. Buford received specific orders to find Lee's army and report back to Meade. However, while conducting his reconnaissance, he faced an unexpected challenge when he observed Confederate troops marching toward strategic high ground.

General John Buford was commander of the 1st Division during the battle of Gettysburg and the senior division commander under General Alfred Pleasanton, the commander of the Army of the Potomac's Cavalry Corps. On June 30th,

Buford received orders to scout the vicinity of Gettysburg and find Lee's army. At about 11:00 am, he set up one mile west of the town, dismounted his cavalry and deployed his artillery blocking the road in response to Confederate skirmishers coming into Gettysburg. Buford's cavalry drove them back; however, the skirmishers report to Confederate General Heth that there was a Union militia in the town. Heth decided that he would not let a mere militia drive him away and decided to retaliate with force. Throughout the night, Buford received reports that indicate the Army of Northern Virginia was massing at Gettysburg and he would send the updates back to Meade, who had not yet picked a location for the battle. As a cavalry commander, Buford was ordered to find Lee's army and report back; he was ordered to not get decisively engaged with the enemy. However, Buford knew that if the Confederates seized control of the high ground around Gettysburg, they would have the tactical advantage throughout the battle. He had to make a decision to withdraw or fight. If he chose to fight, his scouts would soon face the Confederate infantry was marching toward his position. During the Civil War, cavalry units were no match against infantry units. Buford had to decide what to do based on his orders, the strategic high ground around him, and the composition of the enemy.

Up to this point, Buford did the job he was assigned to do, which was find the Confederate Army and report back. He could have withdrawn with the reassurance that he was following orders as well as making a tactically sound decision not to engage Confederate infantry, which would surely destroy his cavalry if he did not receive reinforcements. Since he had no direct communication with his headquarters, he did not know whether the needed reinforcements would come in time. Meade was already in the process of making plans to engage the Army of Northern Virginia and the decision to commit the Union army in a major engagement rested with Meade. If Buford decided to engage, he might run the risk of disrupting Meade's plans. However, as an experienced soldier, Buford knew the importance of the high ground. He knew that if the Confederates were able to seize the high ground around Gettysburg, they would have the tactical advantage; the Confederates could dig in and set up strong defensive positions. Since they were in northern territory, the Union would have no choice but to attack.

Buford sent messengers to report the situation while he made a decision on whether to deploy his entire division and attempt to hold the town until the arrival of the Army of the Potomac's First Corps under the leadership of General John Reynolds or not. At 9:00 a.m. on July 1st, two brigades of General Heth's division attacked and Buford's artillery fired three cannon volleys, thus beginning the Battle of Gettysburg. Buford's men dismounted and in a very short order, he lost 25 percent of his force. However, his cavalry was armed with Spencer repeating rifles, which could shoot faster than the Confederate rifles, which had to be loaded one round at a time. This significant difference in the rate of fire allowed Buford's cavalry to hold off the Confederate attack. At 10:00 a.m., low on ammunition and high on casualties, Buford looked for signs of the Union First Corps. While waiting for First Corps, General Reynolds, commander of the Union left side, arrived and immediately ordered the 11th Corps to Gettysburg, where they would take positions along Cemetery Hill. The First Corps arrived shortly thereafter and relieved Buford's cavalry. With the reinforcements in place, the Union forces maintained control of the important high ground around Gettysburg. Reynolds became the highest casualty of the battle when he was killed by a sniper while he rallied the Union reinforcements. Buford lost 70 percent of his force; however, his actions resulted in the Union forces gaining the most defensible terrain on the battlefield and forced Lee to fight his army piecemeal rather than in mass while he bought time for the Army of the Potomac to mass; Lee did not want the Army of Northern Virginia to be decisively engaged until the entire army was massed around Gettysburg. Buford's decision to fight forced Lee to fight before he was ready.

During this opening battle sequence, Buford demonstrated one of the fundamental elements of leadership - acting in the interest of the greater good. He made decisions based on what was best for the Army of the Potomac, not based on what was best for him. Buford risked the lives of every man in his entire unit, including his own, in order to secure the high ground before reinforcements arrived. Every organization should strive to have a Buford, somebody who can quickly assess a fast moving situation and then make a decision that is best for the organization. Another key element to consider is Buford's reputation. Since Buford was known to be a skilled soldier who acted in the best interest of his unit, his superiors could trust his judgement. When Meade received reports that Buford was holding off the Confederates, Meade quickly moved his army in response instead of getting mad that Buford had chosen to engage the enemy before consulting his higher headquarters because of his reputation. If you want to have the same trust Buford had, you need to have a reputation as a good follower and a demonstrated track record of good judgement. In order for you to cultivate a Buford, you should create an atmosphere that rewards taking the initiative and provides the right experience to every individual, so that people can learn and grow to become a Buford. Finally, you must make sure everybody understands the goals and values of the organization, so that people can make decisions based on the good of the organization. Technology allows us to move faster and faster each day; it is critical you instill the right organizational culture.

Chapter 3: Understanding and giving clear guidance

Clear communication is one of the fundamental tenants of leadership. It does not matter if you have the best idea or plan in the world if you cannot articulate that plan to your team. So many mistakes happen because somebody did not clearly state guidance. One of the best tools to use is a "backbrief" method. The backbrief method is a technique used in the military in which, after receiving instructions, a team member briefs the leader on what he or she believes is the task they have been asked to accomplish. This serves as a great method of making sure your instructions as a leader are clear. If the team member says something that does not match what you intended, you can fix the problem right away instead of finding out when it is too late that your team member did not understand the task.

I have discovered through my professional experience and through surveys given when I have conducted leadership seminars, that too often, managers try to soften tough language to a point that it is hard to understand the real intent. These managers then hide behind such misused leadership axioms such as "it is up to the team members to understand what I really mean" or "suggestions should be taken as commands." These kind of messages are cop outs for soft leaders who fail to do the job of providing clear guidance. Remember, if you are a leader, you are evaluated on the performance of the team. If your team does not understand what you want, then it is your fault. Therefore, why take any chances that your guidance might be misunderstood? State what you want very clearly. Sometimes you might want to defer some decisions to your team members. That is fine, so long as that is what you want. As you will see below, Robert E. Lee worded his guidance in a way to suggest that his subordinate general, General Ewell, had a choice regarding Lee's guidance when in reality, Lee had a particular course of action he wanted Ewell to take.

During the first day of the battle, Lee observed the Federals retreating and saw an opportunity to take the high ground at Culps Hill. He sent orders to Ewell to take the hill "if practicable." As I mentioned in the first chapter, Ewell was fighting his first battle as Corps commander working directly for Lee. Before his promotion, Ewell worked for the recently killed Stonewall Jackon and Jackson always gave him direct orders; Lee was known for a more gentile style which can come off as ambiguous. So when Ewell heard Lee use the phrase "if practicable," Ewell interpreted Lee's guidance as leaving him the choice to take the hill or not depending on Ewell's analysis of the situation.

After fighting most of the day, Ewell decided it was going to be dark soon, his soldiers had been fighting hard, and he did not have a good sense of his unit's status regarding casualties, ammunition, and disposition. He was very uncomfortable ordering an attack when he was not sure if he had enough ammunition and man power to pull it off. He therefore decided not to attack. He figured he could get a status of his men and then launch the attack in the morning. However, Lee had wanted Ewell to take the hill at all cost. Jackson, who was used to Lee's style, would likely have taken the hill. Ewell, who did not have the same relationship with Lee as Jackson had, did not understand Lee's style of giving orders. By the time a furious Lee rode to Ewell's headquarters, the opportunity had past. Lee clearly had a desired outcome, but he failed to convey that point when he added the phrase "if practicable."

The lesson is that as a leader, you are ultimately responsible for the success or failure of your endeavor. Therefore, when you have a new person on the team, do not assume he will understand exactly what you mean. Leading is about relationships. When you have a long association with a person, you develop a clear understanding of what that person means when certain words or phrases are used. When you are new to a relationship, you do not know what a person's tone, gestures, or mannerisms mean. So if you are in charge and a new team member serves in a key junior leadership position, make your guidance as clear as possible. If you want to trust that junior leader to make a call based on that person's assessment of the situation, then you have to accept whatever decision the junior leader makes and its consequences.

Unfortunately, I have observed this disconnect between what leaders communicate versus what they really want in just about every organization of which I have been a part. Sometimes people do not want to come off as being too tyrannical by dictating a specific course of action. Other times, a successful leader with a good track record comes into a new position or receives a new team member, and just assumes everyone is going to know what that leader wants. Remember, at the end of the day, you are the one in charge. As I stated above, as a leader, it is okay to give employees the ability to decide. In fact, that is often the best thing to do because junior leaders serving below you are closer to the action and are capable of making more timely decisions. For instance, let's say Lee really wanted to give Ewell the choice of taking Culp's hill or not based on Ewell's assessment of the situation. If that was the case, Lee would have had to be fine with whatever choice Ewell eventually made, and then trusted Ewell's judgement that he made the best decision based on what he understood as the facts on the ground. Bottom line, if you give somebody the choice to make a decision, do not be critical when they make the choice you feel is incorrect. If you have a specific outcome of a task, then state it very clearly so there is no room for misunderstanding.

Chapter 4: Accountability

Leaders often need to hold junior members of the team accountable for their actions in the event of a mistake. Sometimes leaders have to hold themselves accountable as well. For instance, was the mistake caused by unclear guidance from a leader? Did the leader put the wrong person in charge with a specific task? Accountability can take many forms depending on whether the mistake was made while genuinely trying to do the right thing or if the mistake was the result of negligence. Other things to consider include any personal issues that may have an impact on the team member. When deciding a course of action to take, leaders have to include all relevant information before making a decision. Robert E. Lee did not have full awareness of the Union military positions because his cavalry commander had not been around to provide him with intelligence on the Union locations. The absence of the cavalry is one of the key factors that many historians believe contributed to the defeat at Gettysburg. I will lay out the situation in detail and then show how Lee held his cavalry commander accountable. Keep in mind the reasons Lee made his choice. Would you have done something different?

Confederate Cavalry commander James Ewell Brown (J.E.B.) Stuart is probably one of the most famous generals to ever wear a uniform in U.S. history. He was a brilliant commander with an excellent track record, but he was also known for his vanity and desire for personal glory. Stuart had a very flamboyant style, donning a cape, yellow sash, flower in his lapel, and hat cocked to the side with an ostrich plume sticking out. An easy target for ridicule, his battlefield performance made him a favorite of Lee. Lee had been Stuart's superintendent while at West Point and he was Lee's aid de camp during the mission to capture John Brown at Harper's Ferry.

One month before Gettysburg, Stuart was caught off guard by General Pleasanton's cavalry and lost 500 men just after he held a Grand Review for General Lee. His troops mocked him for it and the press ridiculed him. Unused to this humiliation, Stuart was determined to restore his own glory. He believed his most important task at Gettysburg was to restore his honor and he was therefore not focused on his most important task, which was finding the Union Army and reporting back to Lee. Here again, Lee faced a leadership challenge. He knew Stuart had an independent streak and while that streak made him a success during the many battles in which he humiliated the Army of the Potomac, it also compelled Stuart to pursue courses of action which suited his own self interest. Based on his battlefield history with Stuart, Lee should have understood what was going through the proud mind of Stuart.

In fact, that independent streak made him a success during the many battles in which he humiliated the Army of the Potomac. Like any trait, it can be a double edged sword. On a positive note, such a person is heavily reliable in getting the job done or reacting in the face of adversity. That same trait is detrimental, however, because sometimes the employee will instinctively act in his own best interests. Lee knew Stuart was a very proud man and after the humiliation at Brandy Station, Lee should have been very clear in his expectations to ensure Stuart did not focus too much on trying to redeem his honor.

You will have members of your team, even some of your best performers, who make mistakes. After a mistake, the first thing is to make sure the team member understands the mistake and has a plan to avoid making the same mistake in the future. In addition, you will have to lay clear expectations for the next project and make sure the employee does not try to overcorrect. Your top performers may feel the sting more so than other employees. In their effort to redeem themselves, they may take a path that, while well intentioned, is detrimental to the overall team goals. Remind them that you still have confidence in them but also provide clear guidance so they correctly fulfill the mission.

When dealing with larger than life figures or individuals who have huge egos, you do not necessarily want to tear them down, but you want to appeal to their expertise and accomplishments. After acknowledging past deeds, carefully explain exactly what you want and how his or her role is important to the overall mission.

In choosing his actions, Lee had to consider a few factors. If he fired Stuart, then he would have to find a capable replacement. If he kept Stuart, then Lee would have to face the rumblings of other officers who might say, "Had that been me, I would have been fired, but Stuart is Lee's guy, so nothing is going to happen to him." Stuart was a favorite of Lee's. The easiest way to minimize negative reactions from your subordinates is to explain your decisions. In this case, Lee decided to retain Stuart because he had performed brilliantly in the past. His battlefield exploits were unparalleled and his absence leading up to the battle and through first two days of the battle was party the result of Lee's ineffective communication. In the future, Lee would have to take the time to make sure his guidance is very clear. Stuart would need to take it upon himself to ensure he clearly understands Lee's intent so that he properly performs the needed task.   Lee expressed his extreme displeasure, he then told Stuart that they would never speak of it again and that he needed Stuart's help in defeating the Army of the Potomac. People will make mistakes. They will do things that cost the company money. However, if the person is a good employee, you have to not only express your displeasure at the mistake, you have to build the person up so he can put the incident behind him and succeed in the future.

When a person on your team makes a mistake, consider whether the cause was a result of you poorly communicating your guidance and identify ways to prevent that in the future. Assess the damage of the mistake and whether the team member is somebody who is a good person of character who can learn and grow from the experience. If not, then perhaps you and your team member must part ways. However, if you see this person as somebody who understands the mistake and is willing to accept responsibility and then learn and grow from the mistake, then it is up to you to build them up so they can be the success you expected them to be when you made them part of the team.

Chapter 5: Proactive leadership

How many times have you heard the phrase, "everyone is a leader?" While often quoted, organizations can face difficulties conveying the importance of this idea and how to put this into action. Sometimes there is a disconnect between promoting an idea and implementing it. Employees might be excited about taking on the initiative to make their organization better, but they are not completely sure how to do it. Senior leaders may promote the mission, but may not communicate effectively enough what actions employees must take. Finally, there are cases when employees may understand the goals and strategy, but they are more afraid of making a mistake and getting fired, so they default to taking no action at all. However, proactive leadership is one of the most important norms leaders of organizations must promote. After all, a leader cannot be everywhere. Often times, success comes down to an individual taking a critical action at a critical moment with the absence of immediate guidance. This type of leadership is also known as personal leadership, which is taking responsibility for yourself and if necessary, those around you. It is taking initiative to fix something that you see is wrong or helping somebody who is struggling. Some have argued that personal leadership is really what drives organizations. Jack Welch, former CEO of General Electric, said it is everybody's job to find ways to better the organization, and that is the essence of personal leadership. It is up to leaders to encourage this kind of initiative to improve speed and quality.

Most discussions about the Battle of Gettysburg, indeed the entire civil war, focus on the actions of the commanding generals. Even in this book, I spend a good deal of time discussing what Lee or Meade did or did not do correctly.

However, no matter the merits of the plans and guidance provided by Meade, Lee, or any of the other commanders, Gettysburg may have had a different ending if not for the actions of one man, Union General G.K. Warren. Warren had no command title and he had no legal authority to issue battlefield commands. His role was Chief Engineer and in this position, his job was to advise Meade on the battlefield terrain. In his early engineering career, he took part in studies of possible transcontinental railroad routes and created the first comprehensive map of the United States west of the Mississippi in 1857. When the Civil War started, he was a mathematics instructor at West Point. While a great engineer, he was never known for his great leadership skills. Given his background, most people would never guess that he had a key role in the Union victory at Gettysburg.

After the first day of battle, the Union held the key high ground and so Lee devised a plan to attack the Union positions with a carefully coordinated series of attacks. One of his objectives was to seize control of Little Round Top. While the effort was not as synchronized as planned, Lee had the initiative. Adding to the promise of success were reports from the Confederate General John Bell Hood's scouts that Little Round Top was not occupied. Meanwhile, Meade sent Warren to survey the terrain and so Warren moved to the Union left to watch the heated action in the Wheat Field. On Little Round Top, he noticed Confederate soldiers a mile away beyond Seminary Ridge. He ordered a nearby artillery battery to fire a volley over the heads of the suspected formation. Through his binoculars, he saw the reflection of hundreds of bayonets and realized that these soldiers were about to flank the Union left. Warren had no time to inform Meade and he understood that if the Confederates placed artillery on Little Round Top, the Union would face devastating fire and the Confederates would have the opportunity to break the Union defense. Warren took decisive action and ordered Colonel

Strong Vincent to immediately occupy the position and his forces arrived just minutes before the Confederates began their attack of Little Round Top. Had Warren not acted, the confederates would have been able to defeat the Union left flank and continue the attack against the rest of the Union line. His actions saved the Union from certain defeat and helped ensure the overall Union victory at Gettysburg. What makes this action so significant is that Warren was merely a staff officer and had no command authority. Technically, he was committing an offense subject to court martial due to his lack of command authority. However, in recognition of his actions, he was promoted and given a command following the battle.

Warren's actions highlight the need for organizations to encourage team members to take the initiative. I have always had the philosophy that you can be a leader where ever you are, meaning that you should always take the initiative to find ways to improve your organization. Had Meade not created an atmosphere that rewarded initiative, Warren may not have felt as confident about making such a critical order to solidify the Union defense. This example also demonstrates the importance of ensuring everyone understands the plan and the desired outcome. Had warren not understood the plan, he would not have made such a critical decision at such a critical time.

No matter what your job title, you need to see yourself as a leader. If you are already in a leadership position, you should encourage those under your supervision to see themselves as leaders as well. More experienced people on your team should take it upon themselves to mentor new people and look for ways to make the organization better. Personal leadership involves promoting ideas, helping those on the team, and setting the example. Too many people, especially those who are not supervisors, go to work with blinders on. They only worry about their own project or task and do not consider how they might contribute to improving the organization. As leaders, you can correct this behavior by eliminating fear, instilling trust, and encouraging and rewarding initiative when taken. Warren saw a problem and took action. Not only was this a credit to Warren, but it was a credit to leaders over him who encouraged such behavior. Someone who is more autocratic may have discouraged Warren from taking such a decisive action which played a pivotal role in the Union victory.

Chapter 6: Leaders are made, not born

One of the most hotly debated leadership questions is "are leaders made or born?" While it is true that some people may inherit in born characteristics for leadership, much like a star athlete may have a high degree of natural talent, it is possible to nurture your talents and excel through hard work and dedication. The sports world is filled with athletes who may not have been born an athlete, but with discipline and practice, excelled to become as talented or even more talented than other athletes in the same league. The similar is true with leaders.

The U.S. Military Academy at West Point is one of the best leadership institutions in the world and the academy's philosophy is that leaders are made. Just like a naturally talented athlete, a person with natural leadership abilities should augment those traits with training and ambition; at the same time, people who do not have the natural instincts to lead can learn to lead through many hours of practice, experience, and study. One such individual who rose to become one of the most respected leaders during the Battle of Gettysburg was Joshua Chamberlain.

Joshua Chamberlain was a professor at Baldwin college in Maine when the war started. He requested a leave of absence to join the army. When his request was refused, he asked for and received a sabbatical for a year's study abroad; however, he left the sabbatical and immediately joined the army. Given his education, he rose through the ranks. Unlike most of the other prominent officers, Chamberlain was not a West Point graduate nor did he have any formal military training. Although he was initially intimidated, Chamberlain spent his time mastering his craft by studying and seeking the advice of experts. He would master military tasks step by step and then put them into practice as he mastered them instead of trying to learn everything at once. During his first night as Brigade commander, he would learn some basic commands for marching the soldiers, and then he would stand in front of his brigade and practice those maneuvers. Each night, he learned a new set of maneuvers and the next day, he would employ them with his brigade. His soldiers never guessed that he was only one step ahead of them.

Not only was he a quick study, but one Chamberlain's other strengths was the genuine care he had for his soldiers. One of the first lessons I learned at West Point was "take care of your soldiers and they will take care of you." Chamberlain placed a premium on the welfare of his troops and his troops rewarded him with fierce loyalty. Chamberlain would prove to be a very skilled military tactician, but the care he had for his soldiers is what won them over. It was also one of the reasons that when faced with strong Confederate opposition at Gettysburg, his troops stuck by him.

In the previous chapter, I discussed General Warren's effort to move units to Little Round Top to defend the Union left flank. Chamberlain's regiment, the 20th Maine, was one of those units. The 20th Maine was the far left side; Chamberlain was told that he must hold at all cost. Confederate soldiers charged multiple times; the 20th was getting low on ammunition and high on casualties. Chamberlain later recalled that at one point, they were entirely pushed from their original position and that there were more enemies around him than his own men. On the far left of his position, he watched as his men fired their last shots and then used their rifles as clubs.

Chamberlain knew he could not hold on much longer. However, he knew he could not retreat and he did not have enough ammunition to hold his position. He called his company commanders for a meeting and told them that he wanted all soldiers to fix bayonets; he wanted to charge the Confederate soldiers. He decided that the Confederate units had to be just as tired, low on ammunition, and worn out at his unit. He also decided that the 20th Maine would have the advantage by charging downhill. His subordinate commanders quickly ordered soldiers to fix bayonets and awaited the order to launch the attack. Lt. Melcher, a junior officer in the 20th Maine, moved forward with the unit colors to look over the ledge. However, Captain spears, who cannot hear due to the commotion of the battle, thought the charge had begun and then ordered his own company to charge. The rest of the 20th Maine saw Spears's company charge and they follow suit. Chamberlain then joined the charge.

The 20th Maine captured 300 prisoners and broke the Confederate attack. For his actions at Little Round Top, Chamberlain received the Medal of Honor, the nation's highest military award. Chamberlain never ordered the charge for which history credits him, but it was his plan; although Spears initiated the charge, he followed the intent of Chamberlain. That is why clear guidance is so essential; Spears jumped the gun, but since the entire Brigade understood the plan, there was no hesitation to move forward; had the rest of the 20th Maine hesitated, the charge would have been disjointed and may have failed. This is a perfect example why leaders must provide clear guidance and intent, because there is always confusion in fluid situations. Understanding the big picture, providing clear guidance, and empowering subordinates all contributed to Chamberlain's success. His leadership success drew the attention of Ulysses S. Grant and President Lincoln. Lincoln breveted Chamberlain to the rank of Major General while Grant selected Chamberlain to accept the Confederate surrender at Appomattox Courthouse. Chamberlain epitomizes the notion that leaders are made.

Chapter 7: Disagreeing with your boss

Speaking truth to power, in the sense that you disagree with the idea, instruction, or methodology of a particular task or guidance, is one of the hardest things to do for a leader. After all, disagreement can sometimes result in being fired. Most good senior leaders are willing to let junior leaders initially disagree or even offer a counter proposal; however, after the senior leader hears the initial objections but decides to proceed as planned, the junior leader is supposed to execute as instructed. While this may be true for the most part, you may find yourself in a situation where the consequences of a senior leader's decision are so grave that you have no choice but to put your whole entire career on the line. During the battle of Gettysburg, Confederate General Longstreet faced this challenge in dealing with an order he received from Robert E. Lee.

Gettysburg is regarded as the most famous battle of the Civil War, and within that battle was probably the most infamous military action of the war, and possibly one of the most infamous military actions in the history of Western Civilization - Picket's Charge. Lee believed that the combined force of all the Confederate Artillery followed by a 15,000 man charge directed at the Union center would break the Army of the Potomac, resulting in not only just a battlefield victory, but a victory for the southern cause. However, the Confederate infantry would have to move through just over 3/4 of a mile of open terrain before reaching the Union lines. Historians named the charge after Major General George Pickett, but he was just one division commander involved in the charge, which fell under the overall command of General Longstreet.

During the evening of July 2, Lee summoned Lieutenant General James Longstreet and ordered him to coordinate and lead this charge against the center of the Union forces. Longstreet did not think this was a good idea. In fact, he thought it would be a catastrophic failure. Longstreet knew that Lee's trademark was pulling off seemingly impossible tasks with tremendous success. However, his experience told him that this attack would be a disaster and lead to high casualties. That day, he faced the dilemma of following his orders as a soldier or communicating his objections to his superior.

Longstreet began a rebuttal to Lee but Lee was adamant that the charge would go forward. Longstreet suggested that the Confederate Army move around the Union left flank and position themselves between the Army of the Potomac and Washington, so that Lee would be able to select the ground of his choosing for defense and force the Union to attack him. Lee famously retorted, "General, the enemy is there (Gettysburg), I aim to strike him." Lee was convinced that his plan would succeed and neither Longstreet, or any other general, would convince him otherwise. Longstreet could not see how any positive outcome could result from what he knew deep in his heart to be a suicidal assault, so he summoned all of his courage, indeed, put his entire career on the line, to remind Lee that he had "been a soldier all of his life, commanding units in combat from every echelon from squad to corps, and in his opinion, no 15,000 men in any army could take the Union position." Lee would not hear of it. In a final act of resistance, Longstreet suggested that General A.P. Hill should lead the attack because two of the three divisions making the attack belonged to Hill. This attempt to pass on command to Hill angered Lee, who then told Longstreet his decision to attack was final.

In retrospect, Longstreet professionally laid out his concerns and stated his logic. Most importantly, he did not simply point out a problem with the plan, but also provided a solution that he believed was a better option. So the first lesson of this episode between Lee and Longstreet is that if you disagree with the decision made by somebody in a position of authority, you need to at least have a viable alternative for consideration.

However, sometimes no matter how you persuade the boss, the boss will insist on his course of action. Depending on the topic of discussion and how strongly you feel about the intended action, you could potentially face a dilemma - following the guidance you received or resigning in protest. Each person has to make up his or her own mind based on the circumstances. Just about every leadership class I attended provides a scenario in which you disagree with your boss and the class discusses ways to raise this objection. The school solution is always, "state your objection professionally and logically. However, if the boss still wants to move forward with the plan, then you follow his or her guidance." I believe this is the proper guidance for about 99 percent of the time you may find yourself disagreeing with somebody in a position of higher authority. After all, that is how you want your own subordinates to handle disagreement. There are some instances where the guidance is legally, morally and ethically wrong. The most famous example of this is the Nuremberg trials, in which lower level Nazis tried to use the defense that they were only following orders. The courts decided that what they did was so morally reprehensible that they should have disobeyed those orders. Longstreet found himself in a grayer area. He believed deep in his heart the attack would be a disaster. From a moral standpoint, he did not want to see all those soldiers die for an impossible task. However, he knew Lee had pulled off impossible tasks in the past. Perhaps he would do so again. Everyone has to live with their own choices. In this situation, after raising my objections multiple times, I would have offered my resignation. Thankfully, I have never been in a position where it came down to that. But one day, all of us might. We have to look in our own hearts and make the decision we believe is right.

There is also a lesson here for those in power who receive objections from subordinates about their guidance. Lee gave Longstreet his position as Corps Commander because he trusted his tactical judgement. Lee often referred to Longstreet as "my old war horse." When a trusted subordinate comes to you with an objection, that is not something that should easily be dismissed. You may ultimately dismiss their objection or alternative idea. Before doing so though, seriously ponder the reasons you put that person in such a position. That person is there because he/she has a track record of success and sound judgement. Subordinate leaders are also more in touch with the "facts on the ground" than a more senior leader. The senior leader often has a better understanding of the vision or bigger picture. Should Lee have listened to Longstreet? History suggests he should have. It is unclear how seriously Lee considered Longstreet's alternative idea. Longstreet's idea to bypass Meade and select a strategic piece of ground to defend that was located between Meade and Washington, D.C. made more sense given that it is very hard to attack dug in positions. It is also easier to defend against a force of superior size than it is to attack one. This was Lee's call to make and he decided to stand firm by the soundness of his plan. As a leader, you need a Longstreet who is not afraid to tell you what he thinks. You, of course, will always make the final call, but when a Longstreet raises a concern, you should consider what he says very seriously. General Robert E. Lee was a dramatic success in the past, but, as history showed us at Gettysburg, past success is not always an indicator of future success.

As most people know from history, Picket's charge was a disaster. The Confederate artillery barrage that was supposed to destroy the Union artillery prior to the assault failed. The Confederate guns were missing their targets but, due to the smoke, the Confederate artillery commanders could not see very well. Union generals quickly realized that the Confederates were using their artillery to disable the Union artillery, so they ordered the guns silent so the Confederates would think they destroyed the Union artillery and launch the assault. This left the Confederates vulnerable as they marched into what became the full storm of Union artillery. Despite the deadly Union artillery fire, some Confederate soldiers were able breach the low stone wall that shielded many of the Union defenders. However, this was not enough and ultimately the Confederates could not hold this position and were repulsed with over 50 percent casualties and forced to withdraw. A famous account states that during the withdrawal, Lee ordered General Picket to order his division to occupy a defensive position, afraid the Union would counterattack. Pickett responded to Lee by stating, "General Lee, I have no division!" He had lost all his men.

Finally, Pickett's charge is also an example of a senior leader having obsolete ideas. Tourists and scholars who visit Gettysburg are confused as to why Lee would order a charge across such open ground; however, Lee studied the tactics of Napoleon Bonaparte at West Point. Pickett's charge made sense when considering those tactics. Lee attacked the Union right on the first day and the union left on the second day. In each case, the Meade moved soldiers from the center to reinforce the respective sides. The center was therefore the weakest point in the Union line. However, rifles and cannons were far more effective than they were during the era of Napoleon. So while the center was weak, the Confederates would have to cross open terrain and would be subjected to deadly fire while crossing that ground. So leaders must make sure that their ideas are relevant.

Chapter 8: Leading by example

Leading by example is one of the best traits any leader can possess. Any leader can order or instruct somebody to do a task or behave in a particular manner, but the best leaders never ask anyone to do anything that they would not do themselves. Leaders also are able to make better decisions by understanding the conditions under which their team members are working. Sometimes when faced in a chaotic situation, just seeing a leader doing a certain act is enough to get the rest of the team to follow. Leading by example is important at every level, but especially for younger executives, since younger executives are more visible to the workforce. Some every day examples of leading by example include being the first one in the office and the last one to leave; setting the standard for professional dress; staying late in the office when you know your team has to work late. These examples earn you a tremendous measure of respect. When team members see your example, they respect you more and are drawn closer to you. While Gettysburg has many examples of leading by example, I will highlight two very important ones here.

General Lewis A. Armistad led one of Pickett's brigades during the infamous Pickett's charge. As the Confederate charge stalled, he put his hat on top of his sword so that his men could see where he was in the confusion of the battlefield. Not only was he present with his soldiers, but he was out front leading them. His unit would penetrate the deepest of all the Confederate troops into the Federal Line at the Angle, which is also referred to as the "high water mark" of the Confederacy. Without that symbolic gesture, his unit would have remained disorganized and would not have penetrated as far as it did.

In a chaotic situation, the presence of the leader helps keep the rest of the organization calm and focused.

During that same charge, General Winfield Scott Hancock wanted to demonstrate to his corps that he was standing side by side his men. Sitting gallantly on his horse, he rode up and down the line encouraging each soldier. When one of his brigade commanders told him, "General, the corps commander ought not to risk his life that way." Hancock replied, "There are times when a corps commander's life does not count." Hancock knew that during this point in the battle, the soldiers already knew their orders. It was up to the leaders to encourage them and keep their morale high. Certainly the soldiers at the Union center, watching their corps commander remain calmly on his horse, were more motivated knowing that their leader shared in their sacrifice and was willing to put his own life at risk.

In the confusion and chaos of battle, both of these leaders kept their units focused by making a clear signal that they were in charge and that they were not only present, but actively leading their units. While it it my hope that the reader does not find himself or herself in battle, there are probably times you will find yourself in a chaotic situation. It is during these times that you must be present at the decisive point. It may be as simple as coming to the office late at night when your team is working on a tight deadline. Even if you are not actively guiding the team, your presence can boost the morale, especially if you bring in some comfort food. Your presence is also a signal that you are sharing the hardship of your employees by sacrificing your own time just as they are. Most importantly, when you face a situation when you need your employees to make a sacrifice to accomplish a tight deadline or stay late to fulfill a key task, I guarantee it will not be the last time you will require such an effort. If, during the first instance you demonstrate your willingness to sacrifice your personal time to be with your employees, you will minimize, or possibly eliminate, any complaints when you have to do it another time.

Chapter 9: Having a backup plan

When it comes to planning, you must always have a backup option. In sports, the loss of a key player can turn a championship caliber team into a loser if there is not an adequately trained replacement. In business, it is essential to think about secondary alternatives should the first plan not work out. The backup plan should be understood at every level of the organization so anybody can act if needed. Furthermore, everyone at every level of an organization should develop alternative courses of action. Fortunately for Lee, while JEB Stuart's cavalry was not providing the intelligence information Lee needed, Longstreet had a backup option in the form of Harrison, a former actor turned spy.

Harrison, only known by his last name, found the Union Army and told Longstreet that the Union army had crossed the Potomac River and was between Washington, D.C. and Lee's army. He also added that there were seven Union corps coming after Lee. However, while Harrison's information was accurate, Lee refused to believe it because Lee did not care for spies and that if Harrison was telling the truth, surely JEB Stuart would have provided that information. Thus, Lee delayed making any battle plans. Finally, Longstreet eventually persuaded Lee by pointing out that Stuart had provided no information. Lee reluctantly decided to accept Harrison's information. Had Longstreet not seen the utility of Harrison, it is likely that the confederate army would have been caught by complete surprise and the battle might have ended much quicker and costlier for the Confederates. However, Lee's refusal to accept Harrison's report did cost Lee the initiative. Lee could have moved his forces into an advantageous position much quicker had he been more receptive to the information. Therefore, it is important that if your primary option fails, which was the case for Lee, it is essential that you go to the backup plan as soon as possible in order to not lose valuable time. Lee's resistance to accepting the information provided by Harrison leads to another lesson, which is that sometimes you have to challenge your assumptions. It is not clear why Lee did not care for spies. Perhaps it was because he thought the art was ungentlemanly or he had bad experiences in the past. However, had he been more open-minded, he would have been able to react quicker to the information Harrison provided. Longstreet later sent Harrison into the town of Gettysburg to gather more information but disappeared.

Chapter 10: Critiquing success

It is often said that success has a million fathers while failure only has one. Everybody wants to join in the victory celebration and highlight how they somehow contributed to that success. In times of failure, everyone tries to distance themselves from that failure and there is usually an investigation to understand why something failed. However, sometimes you have to critique something that was actually successful. During the Battle of Gettysburg, General Meade accomplished what no other Union general managed to accomplish up to this point - he defeated Robert E. Lee. As Lee's army retreated from the Battlefield, Meade had an opportunity to pursue Lee. The Army of Northern Virginia was defeated, tired, low on ammunition, and high on casualties. Lee's army would also have to make a dangerous crossing across the Potomac River before returning to southern territory. However, Meade knew that Lee was a master strategist and tactician. Lee's cannons were still pointed at the Union Army and Meade had to consider that Lee could set a trap by digging in and using the advantage of a defensive position to inflict high casualties on the Army of the Potomac, and then possibly counterattack. Meade also had to consider the condition of his own army and whether it was in any condition to transition to the offense. President Lincoln felt that Lee's defeat, coupled with him being trapped by the Potomac, presented a golden opportunity to end the war. One of Meade's subordinate commanders, General Alfred Pleasonton, said, "I will give you a half hour to show yourself a great general. Order the army to advance, while I take the cavalry and get in Lee's rear, and we will finish the campaign in a week." Meade responded with "we have done enough." Meade's army had fought a battle of significant consequences and he held his ground.

Lincoln was furious that Meade did not pursue Lee as he retreated. He sent several messages demanding Meade pursue Lee and yet Meade would not budge. It turned out that Meade could have made his move against Lee anytime over the next 10 days, but still chose not to pursue Lee and lost a golden opportunity. Meade was hurt and surprised by Lincoln's angry messages; from Meade's standpoint, he had driven the "Confederate invaders" from Union territory and instead of accolades, Lincoln sent messages criticizing him. The letters were so harsh that Meade at one point asked to be relieved of command.

I believe Lincoln was correct in demanding that Meade finish off Lee's army; however, Lincoln, from his vantage point in Washington, did not have a full appreciation of the intense fighting Meade's army faced. While Meade did not pursue Lee and Lincoln needed to make his disappointment clear, he should have also congratulated Meade on being the first Union commander to defeat Lee. Lincoln may have had better results if he sent an initial message of congratulations and then followed up with a separate message suggesting that now was the time to end the war once and for all. Lincoln was the Commander in Chief. Despite not having a full appreciation of the intense fighting, he understood the importance of delivering a decisive blow to Lee's army and ending the war. Lee escaped and the war would last 22 months, costing thousands of lives. Despite Lincoln's disappointment, Lincoln kept Meade in his position as leader of the Army of the Potomac even after Ulysses S. Grant became the overall Union Commander.

Lincoln's final act on the matter of Gettysburg was a harsh letter he wrote to Meade in which Lincoln admonished Meade for not having the proper strategic understanding regarding the importance of finishing off Lee at Gettysburg. After writing the letter, Lincoln put the letter in his desk and never sent it. This act served two purposes. First, it allowed Lincoln to vent his anger. Secondly, it saved Lincoln from further humiliating a general who, after all, was the first Union commander to defeat Lee. In today's business world, this is like drafting an email but then having the self disciple to not send it. I know I have used this "draft message" technique to blow off steam. Such a technique allows the writer to vent off that initial frustration; however, by not sending the message, you do not make a situation worse by saying something you regret. It really does work and makes you look better in the end.

Chapter 11: Conclusion:

As you can see, everything in leadership stems from communication. With that in mind, consider the following highlights:

1. Always state your intent clearly, with a desired outcome. The clarity of how you state your intent will allow your team members to meet your expectations even as the unexpected arises.

2. Carefully consider whether you want to give your team members the power to decide a course of action or if there is a specific task you want accomplished. If you want something specific, clearly state it so that there is no confusion.

3. Hold people accountable for their actions. That does not mean you always have to punish or fire somebody who makes a mistake, although such actions are certainly on the table. Consider that person's track record and whether he or she can learn from that mistake and emerge as a better person.

4. Encourage proactive leadership. Remind your team that regardless of title, everyone should seek to be a leader no matter where they are in the organizational structure. If you are not yet a leader in title, always look for ways to demonstrate leadership by suggesting a new idea or mentoring a new member of the team.

5. Leaders are made, not born. While there are certainly people with natural talents, with hard work, training, and

experience, anybody can emerge as a Joshua Chamberlain.

6. Never be afraid to tell the truth to your boss. Remember to always have an alternative idea if you are critiquing the plan. Use tact, and explain your position clearly. If you are in a position of power and a trusted person is telling you that your idea or plan is bad, consider what that person is saying very carefully. After all, he or she is also smart and has some unique experience. Ultimately, though, you are in charge and the decision is yours.

7. Lead by example and never ask anybody to do anything that you would never do yourself. Be the first one at work and the last one to leave.

8. Always have a back up plan because you never know when things will go wrong. By having a well crafted back up plan in advance, you can react much faster.

9. Even if you successfully accomplish a task, oftentimes success resulted due to luck as well as preparation. Perhaps you could have emerged even more successful that you did. Analyze the results carefully and honestly critique what you may have done better.

I hope you found this book interesting and that it not only helped you have a better understanding of what happened during those three days at Gettysburg 150 years ago, but that you can take these leadership lessons and apply them to your everyday use. Thank you for taking time to read this and good luck.

About the Author:

Tom Coyle is the President and Founder of Adventures in
Leadership, a leadership development and cross cultural
communication program for business professionals and
students. Tom is a 1997 graduate of the U.S. Military
Academy at West Point and served seven years in the Army
as an artillery officer with the 101st Airborne Division and 3rd
Infantry Division. He then served as a Foreign Service Officer
(FSO) for the U.S. Department of State, where he was posted
in Afghanistan and Bosnia. He is an avid reader and outdoor
adventurer. To find out more about Tom and his company,
visit www.adventuresnleadership.com.

Made in the USA
Middletown, DE
14 July 2024

57261688R00027